my work
attempts to ferret out
what i know & touch
in a woman's body . . .

i discuss the simple reality
of going home at nite,
of washing one's body,
looking out the window
with a woman's eyes.
we must learn our common symbols,
preen them
and share them with the world.
                    —Ntozake Shange

Bantam Books by Ntozake Shange

FOR COLORED GIRLS WHO HAVE CONSIDERED
SUICIDE/WHEN THE RAINBOW IS ENUF
NAPPY EDGES

for colored girls who
have considered suicide/
when the rainbow is enuf

a choreopoem/
ntozake shange

BANTAM BOOKS
Toronto / New York / London

*This low-priced Bantam Book
has been completely reset in a type face
designed for easy reading, and was printed
from new plates. It contains the complete
text of the original hard-cover edition.*
NOT ONE WORD HAS BEEN OMITTED.

FOR COLORED GIRLS WHO HAVE CONSIDERED
SUICIDE WHEN THE RAINBOW IS ENUF

*A Bantam Book / published by arrangement with
Macmillan Publishing Co., Inc.*

PRINTING HISTORY

*Macmillan edition published May 1977
6 printings through January 1979*

Literary Guild edition October 1977

| Bantam edition / January 1980 | |
| 2nd printing .... January 1980 |
| 3rd printing .... March 1980 |
| 4th printing .... August 1981 |

---

*Bantam Books are published by Bantam Books, Inc. Its trade-
mark, consisting of the words "Bantam Books" and the por-
trayal of a bantam, is Registered in U.S. Patent and Trademark
Office and in other countries. Marca Registrada. Bantam
Books, Inc., 666 Fifth Avenue, New York, New York 10103.*

---

for the spirits of my grandma
viola benzena murray owens
and my great aunt
effie owens josey

For Colored Girls Who Have Considered Suicide/When the Rainbow Is Enuf was produced in New York by Joseph Papp and Woodie King, Jr., under the direction of Oz Scott, at the Henry Street Settlement's New Federal Theatre, the New York Shakespeare Festival Public Theatre, and then at the Booth Theatre on Broadway where it opened on September 15, 1976 with the following cast:

Lady in Brown	Janet League
Lady in Yellow	Aku Kadogo
Lady in Red	Trazana Beverley
Lady in Green	Paula Moss
Lady in Purple	Risë Collins
Lady in Blue	Laurie Carlos
Lady in Orange	Ntozake Shange

Scenery by Ming Cho Lee; lighting by Jennifer Tipton; costumes by Judy Dearing; choreography by Paula Moss; music for "I Found God in Myself" by Diana Wharton. Associate Producer, Bernard Gersten. A New York Shakespeare Festival Production in association with the Henry Street Settlement's New Federal Theatre.

poems by title

*for colored girls who have considered suicide/when
the rainbow is enuf* was first presented at the Bac-
chanal, a woman's bar just outside Berkeley, Cali-
fornia. With Paula Moss & Elvia Marta who worked
with me in Raymond Sawyer's Afro-American Dance
Company & Halifu's The Spirit of Dance; Nashira
Ntosha, a guitarist & program coordinator at KPOO-
FM (one of the few Bay Area stations focusing on
women's programming); Jessica Hagedorn, a poet &
reading tour companion; & Joanna Griffin, co-founder
of the Bacchanal, publisher of Effie's Press, & a poet.
We just did it. Working in bars waz a circumstantial
aesthetic of poetry in San Francisco from Spec's, an
old beat hangout, to 'new' Malvina's, Minnie's Can-
Do Club, the Coffee Gallery, & the Rippletad. With
as much space as a small studio on the Lower East
Side, the five of us, five women, proceeded to dance,
make poems, make music, make a woman's theater for
about twenty patrons. This was December of 1974.
We were a little raw, self-conscious, & eager. What-
ever we were discovering in ourselves that nite had
been in process among us for almost two years.

I first met Jessica & Nashira thru Third World Com-
munications (The Woman's Collective) when the first
anthology of Third World women writers in the
U.S.A. was published. With Janice Mirikitani,

Avotcja, Carol Lee Sanchez, Janet Campbell Hale, Kitty Tsui, Janic Cobb, Thulani, and a score more, San Francisco waz inundated with women poets, women's readings, & a multilingual woman presence, new to all of us & desperately appreciated. The force of these readings on all our lives waz to become evident as we directed our energies toward clarifying our lives—& the lives of our mothers, daughters, & grandmothers—as women. During the same period, Shameless Hussy Press & The Oakland Women's Press Collective were also reading anywhere & everywhere they could. In a single season, Susan Griffin, Judy Grahn, Barbara Gravelle, & Alta, were promoting the poetry & presence of women in a legendary malepoet's environment. This is the energy & part of the style that nurtured *for colored girls . . .*

More stable as a source of inspiration & historical continuity waz the Women's Studies Program at Sonoma State College, where I worked with J. J. Wilson, Joanna Griffin, & Wopo Holup over a three year span. Courses designed to make women's lives & dynamics familiar to us, such as: Woman as Artist; Woman as Poet; Androgynous Myths in Literature; Women's Biography I & II; Third World Women Writers, are inextricably bound to the development of my sense of the world, myself, & women's language.

Studying the mythology of women from antiquity
to the present day led directly to the piece *Sechita* in
which a dance hall girl is perceived as deity, as slut, as
innocent & knowing. Unearthing the mislaid, for-
gotten, &/or misunderstood women writers, painters,
mothers, cowgirls, & union leaders of our pasts proved
to be both a supportive experience & a challenge not
to let them down, not to do less than—at all costs not
be less woman than—our mothers, from Isis to Marie
Laurencin, Zora Neale Hurtson to Kathe Kollwitz,
Anna May Wong to Calamity Jane.

Such joy & excitement I knew in Sonoma, then I
would commute back the sixty miles to San Francisco
to study dance with Raymond Sawyer, Ed Mock, &
Halifu. Knowing a woman's mind & spirit had been
allowed me, with dance I discovered my body more
intimately than I had imagined possible. With the
acceptance of the ethnicity of my thighs & backside,
came a clearer understanding of my voice as a woman
& as a poet. The freedom to move in space, to demand
of my own sweat a perfection that could continually
be approached, though never known, waz poem to
me, my body & mind ellipsing, probably for the first
time in my life. Just as Women's Studies had rooted
me to an articulated female heritage & imperative, so
dance as explicated by Raymond Sawyer & Ed Mock

insisted that everything African, everything halfway, colloquial, a grimace, a strut, an arched back over a yawn, waz mine. I moved what waz my unconscious knowledge of being in a colored woman's body to my known everydayness. The depth of my past waz made tangible to me in Sawyer's *Ananse*, a dance exploring the Diaspora to contemporary Senegalese music, pulling ancient trampled spirits out of present tense Afro-American Dance. Watching Ed Mock re-create the Step Brothers' or Bert Williams' routines in class or on stage, in black face mimicking Eddie Cantor or Gloria Swanson, being the rush of irony & control that are the foundation of jazz dance, was as startling as humbling. With Raymond Sawyer & Ed Mock, Paula Moss & I learned the wealth of our bodies, if we worked, if we opened up, if we made the dance our own.

The first experience of women's theater for me as a performer waz the months I spent with Halifu Osumare's The Spirit of Dance, a troupe of five to six black women who depicted the history of Black dance from its origins in Western Africa thru to the popular dances seen on our streets. Without a premeditated or conscious desire to create a female piece, that's what, in fact, Halifu did. Working in San Francisco & Berkeley public schools as an adjunct to

Ethnic Studies, I learned the mechanics of self-production & absorbed some of Halifu's confidence in her work, the legitimacy of our visions. After some 73 performances with The Spirit of Dance, I left the company to begin production of *for colored girls . . .*

In the summer of 1974 I had begun a series of seven poems, modeled on Judy Grahn's *The Common Woman*, which were to explore the realities of seven different kinds of women. They were numbered pieces: the women were to be nameless & assume hegemony as dictated by the fullness of their lives. The first of the series is the poem, 'one' (orange butterflies & aqua sequins), which prompted the title *& this is for colored girls who have considered suicide/when the rainbow is enuf*. I waz smitten by my own language, & called all the performances I waz to give from then on by that title. In other words, all the readings & choreopoetry that Paula Moss & I developed after that summer waz *for colored girls. . . .* We started at the Bacchanal & worked through the winter at Ed Mock's Dance Studio with the assistance of West Coast Dance Works, setting pieces & cleaning up poems. I found two bands, The Sound Clinic (a horn trio) & Jean Desarmes & His Raggae Blues Band, who agreed to work with us if I found space. & I did. The space we used waz the space I knew:

Women's Studies Departments, bars, cafes, & poetry centers. With the selection of poems changing, dependent upon our audience & our mood, & the dance growing to take space of its own, so that Paula inspired my words to fall from me with her body, & The Sound Clinic working with new arrangements of Ornette Coleman compositions & their own, The Raggae Blues Band giving Caribbean renditions of Jimi Hendrix & Redding, we set dates for Minnie's Can-Do Club in Haight-Ashbury. The poets showed up for us, the dancers showed up for us, the women's community showed up, & we were listed as a 'must see' in *The Bay Guardian*. Eight days after our last weekend at Minnie's, Paula & I left to drive cross country to New York to do 'the show,' as we called it, at the Studio Rivbea in New York.

Our work in San Francisco waz over. With the courage of children, we staged the same sort of informal & improvised choreopoems at Rivbea during the Summer Music Festival. Instead of the Standing-Room-Only crowds we were accustomed to in San Francisco, my family & a few friends came to see our great project. One of these friends, Oz Scott, & my sister, Ifa Iyaun, who were instrumental in the development of *for colored girls* . . . saw the show that night. Oz offered to help me with the staging of the work for a New York audience, since Paula & I obviously didn't understand some things. We moved from the Rivbea to the Old Reliable on East 3rd Street to work through some of the ideas Oz had & the new things Paula & I were developing.

Gylan Kain of the Original Last Poets waz working there every Monday night. We worked with him & any other poets & dancers who showed up. Several members of the original New York show came to us just this haphazardly. Aku Kadogo & I both had scholarships at Diane McIntyre's Sounds-in-Motion Dance Studio. I asked her if she felt like improvising on the Lower East Side, she agreed & has been with the show ever since. Laurie Carlos stopped by one evening. She stayed. Somehow word got out & people started coming to the back room of this neighborhood bar. We were moved to a new bar down the street, DeMonte's, after eleven weeks of no-pay hard-work three sets a night—maybe a shot of cognac on the house.

The show at DeMonte's waz prophetic. By this time, December of 1975, we had weaned the piece of ex-traneous theatricality, enlisted Trazana Beverley, Laurie Carlos, Laurie Hayes, Aku Kadogo, & of course, Paula & I were right there. The most prescient change in the concept of the work waz that I gave up directorial powers to Oz Scott. By doing this, I acknowledged that the poems & the dance worked on their own to do & be what they were. As opposed to viewing the pieces as poems, I came to understand these twenty-odd poems as a single statement, a choreopoem.

We finally hit at DeMonte's. Those institutions I had shunned as a poet—producers, theaters, actresses, & sets—now were essential to us. *for colored girls who have considered suicide/when the rainbow is enuf* waz a theater piece. Woody King picked up our option to produce us as a Workshop under Equity's Showcase Code at Henry Street. With the assistance of the New York Shakespeare Festival & Joe Papp, we received space & a set, lights & a mailing list, things Paula & I had done without for two years. We opened at Henry Street with two new actress-dancers Thea Martinez & Judy Dearing. Lines of folks & talk all over the Black & Latin community propelled us to the Public Theater in June. Then to the Booth Theater on Broadway in September of 1976.

Every move we've made since the first showing of *for colored girls* . . . in California has demanded changes of text, personnel, & staging. The final production at the Booth is as close to distilled as any of

us in all our art forms can make it. With two new
actresses, Janet League & Rise Collins, & with the
help of Seret Scott, Michelle Shay, & Roxanne Reese,
the rest of the cast is enveloping almost 6,000 people
a week in the words of a young black girl's growing
up, her triumphs & errors, our struggle to become all
that is forbidden by our environment, all that is for-
feited by our gender, all that we have forgotten.

I had never imagined not doing *for colored girls*. . . .
It waz just my poems, any poems I happened to have.
Now I have left the show on Broadway, to write
poems, stories, plays, my dreams. *for colored girls* . . .
is either too big for my off-off Broadway taste, or too
little for my exaggerated sense of freedom, held over
from seven years of improvised poetry readings. Or,
perhaps, the series has actually finished itself. Poems
come on their own time: i am offering these to you
as what i've received from this world so far.

*i am on the other side of the rainbow/picking up the
pieces of days spent waitin for the poem to be heard/
while you listen/i have other work to do/*

ntozake shange
new york, 1976

for colored girls who
have considered suicide/
when the rainbow is enuf

*The stage is in darkness.
Harsh music is heard as
dim blue lights come up.
One after another, seven
women run onto the stage
from each of the exits.
They all freeze in postures
of distress. The follow spot
picks up the lady in brown.
She comes to life and looks
around at the other ladies.
All of the others are still.
She walks over to the lady
in red and calls to her. The
lady in red makes no re-
sponse.*

    lady in brown
dark phrases of womanhood
of never havin been a girl
half-notes scattered
without rhythm/no tune
distraught laughter fallin
over a black girl's shoulder
it's funny/it's hysterical
the melody-less-ness of her dance

don't tell nobody don't tell a soul
she's dancin on beer cans & shingles

this must be the spook house
another song with no singers
lyrics/no voices
& interrupted solos
unseen performances

are we ghouls?
children of horror?
the joke?

don't tell nobody don't tell a soul
are we animals? have we gone crazy?

i can't hear anythin
but maddening screams
& the soft strains of death
& you promised me
you promised me . . .
somebody/anybody
sing a black girl's song
bring her out
to know herself
to know you
but sing her rhythms

carin/struggle/hard times
sing her song of life
she's been dead so long
closed in silence so long
she doesn't know the sound
of her own voice
her infinite beauty
she's half-notes scattered
without rhythm/no tune
sing her sighs
sing the song of her possibilities
sing a righteous gospel
the makin of a melody
let her be born
let her be born
& handled warmly.

　　lady in brown
i'm outside chicago

　　lady in yellow
i'm outside detroit

　　lady in purple
i'm outside houston

　　lady in red
i'm outside baltimore

lady in green
i'm outside san francisco

lady in blue
i'm outside manhattan

lady in orange
i'm outside st. louis

lady in brown
& this is for colored girls who have considered suicide
but moved to the ends of their own rainbows.

everyone
mama's little baby likes shortnin, shortnin,
mama's little baby likes shortnin bread
mama's little baby likes shortnin, shortnin,
mama's little baby likes shortnin bread

little sally walker, sittin in a saucer
rise, sally, rise, wipe your weepin eyes
an put your hands on your hips
an let your backbone slip
o, shake it to the east
o, shake it to the west
shake it to the one
that you like the best

lady in purple
you're it

>   'As the lady in brown tags
>   each of the other ladies
>   they freeze. When each
>   one has been tagged the
>   lady in brown freezes. Im-
>   mediately "Dancing in the
>   Streets" by Martha and
>   the Vandellas is heard. All
>   of the ladies start to dance.
>   The lady in green, the
>   lady in blue, and the lady
>   in yellow do the pony, the
>   big boss line, the swim,
>   and the nose dive. The
>   other ladies dance in place.

   lady in yellow
it was graduation nite & i waz the only virgin in
      the crowd
bobby mills martin jerome & sammy yates eddie
      jones & randi
all cousins
all the prettiest niggers in this factory town
carried me out wit em
in a deep black buick

   5

smellin of thunderbird & ladies in heat
we rambled from camden to mount holly
laughin at the afternoon's speeches
& danglin our tassles from the rear view mirror
climbin different sorta project stairs
movin toward snappin beer cans &
GET IT GET IT THAT'S THE WAY TO DO IT
    MAMA
all mercer county graduated the same nite
            cosmetology secretarial pre-college
               autoshop & business
all us movin from mama to what ever waz out there

that nite we raced a big ol truck from the barbeque
    stand
trying to tell him bout the party at jacqui's
where folks graduated last year waz waitin to hit it
    wid us
i got drunk & cdnt figure out
whose hand waz on my thigh/but it didn't matter
cuz these cousins martin eddie sammy jerome & bobby
waz my sweethearts alternately since the seventh
    grade
& everybody knew i always started cryin if somebody
    actually
tried to take advantage of me
          at jacqui's

6

ulinda mason was stickin her mouth all out
while we tumbled out the buick
eddie jones waz her lickin stick
but i knew how to dance
                it got soo hot
vincent ramos puked all in the punch
& harly jumped all in tico's face
cuz he was leavin for the navy in the mornin
hadda kick ass so we'd all remember how bad he waz
seems like sheila & marguerite waz fraid
to get their hair turnin back
so they laid up against the wall
lookin almost sexy
didnt wanna sweat
but me & my fellas   we waz dancin

since 1963 i'd won all kinda contests
wid the cousins at the POLICE ATHLETIC LEAGUE
        DANCES
all mercer county knew
any kin to martin yates cd turn somersaults
fore smokey robinson cd get a woman excited

                        The Dells singing "Stay"
                        is heard

we danced   doin nasty ol tricks

*The lady in yellow sings
along with the Dells for a
moment. The lady in
orange and the lady in blue
jump up and parody the
lady in yellow and the
Dells. The lady in yellow
stares at them. They sit
down.*

doin nasty ol tricks i'd been thinkin since may
cuz graduation nite had to be hot
& i waz the only virgin
so i hadda make like my hips waz inta some business
that way everybody thot whoever was gettin it
was a older man cdnt run the streets wit youngsters
martin slipped his leg round my thigh
the dells bumped "stay"
up & down—up & down the new carver homes
WE WAZ GROWN
     WE WAZ FINALLY GROWN

ulinda alla sudden went crazy
went over to eddie cursin & carryin on
tearin his skin wid her nails
the cousins tried to talk sense to her
tried to hold her arms

lissin bitch sammy went on
bobby whispered i shd go wit him
fore they go ta cuttin
fore the police arrived
we teetered silently thru the parkin lot
no un uhuh
we didn't know nothin bout no party
bobby started lookin at me
yeah
he started looking at me real strange
like i waz a woman or somethin/
started talkin real soft
in the backseat of that ol buick
WOW
by daybreak
i just cdnt stop grinnin.

The Dells singing "Stay"
comes in and all of the
ladies except the lady in
blue join in and sing along.

    lady in blue
you gave it up in a buick?

    lady in yellow
yeh, and honey, it was wonderful.

9

> *lady in green*
we used to do it all up in the dark
in the corners . . .

> *lady in blue*
some niggah sweating all over you.

> *lady in red*
it was good!

> *lady in blue*
i never did like to grind.

> *lady in yellow*
what other kind of dances are there?

> *lady in blue*
mambo, bomba, merengue

when i waz sixteen i ran off to the south bronx
cuz i waz gonna meet up wit willie colon
& dance all the time
                    mamba bomba merengue

> *lady in yellow*
do you speak spanish?

10

lady in blue

olà

my papa thot he was puerto rican & we wda been
cept we waz just reglar niggahs wit hints of spanish
so off i made it to this 36 hour marathon dance
con salsa con ricardo
'suggggggggggggar' ray on southern blvd
next door to this fotografi place
jammed wit burial weddin & communion relics
next door to la real ideal genuine spanish barber
            up up up up up stairs & stairs & lotsa hallway
wit my colored new jersey self
didn't know what anybody waz saying
cept if dancin waz proof of origin
                i was jibarita herself that nite
& the next day
i kept smilin & right on steppin
if he cd lead i waz ready to dance
if he cdnt lead
i caught this attitude
                i'd seen rosa do
& wd not be bothered
i waz twirlin hippin givin much quik feet
& bein a mute cute colored puerto rican
til saturday afternoon when the disc-jockey say
'SORRY FOLKS WILLIE COLON AINT GONNA
    MAKE IT TODAY'

& alla my niggah temper came outta control
& i wdnt dance wit nobody
& i talked english loud
& i love you more than i waz mad
uh huh uh huh
more than more than
when i discovered archie shepp & subtle blues
doncha know i wore out the magic of juju
heroically resistin being possessed

oooooooooooooooh the sounds
sneakin in under age to slug's
to stare ata real 'artiste'
& every word outta imamu's mouth waz gospel
& if jesus cdnt play a horn like shepp
waznt no need for colored folks to bear no cross at all

& poem is my thank-you for music
& i love you more than poem
more than aureliano buendia loved macondo
more than hector lavoe loved himself
more than the lady loved gardenias
more than celia loves cuba or graciela loves el son
more than the flamingoes shoo-do-n-doo-wah love
    bein pretty

oyè négro
te amo mas que   te amo mas que
when you play
yr flute

    everyone (very softly)
te amo mas que   te amo mas que

    lady in red
without any assistance or guidance from you
i have loved you assiduously for 8 months 2 wks &
    a day
i have been stood up four times
i've left 7 packages on yr doorstep
forty poems 2 plants & 3 handmade notecards i left
town so i cd send to you have been no help to me
on my job
you call at 3:00 in the mornin on weekdays
so i cd drive 27½ miles cross the bay before i go to
    work
charmin charmin
but you are of no assistance
i want you to know
this waz an experiment
to see how selfish i cd be

13

if i wd really carry on to snare a possible lover
if i waz capable of debasin my self for the love of
      another
if i cd stand not being wanted
when i wanted to be wanted
& i cannot
so
with no further assistance & no guidance from you
i am endin this affair

this note is attached to a plant
i've been waterin since the day i met you
you may water it
yr damn self

    lady in orange
i dont wanna write
in english or spanish
i wanna sing   make you dance
like the bata   dance   scream
twitch hips wit me cuz
i done forgot all abt words
aint got no definitions
i wanna whirl
        with you

*Music starts, "Che Che
Cole" by Willie Colon.
Everyone starts to dance.*

our whole body
wrapped like a ripe mango
ramblin whippin thru space
on the corner in the park
where the rug useta be
let willie colon take you out
swing your head
push your leg to the moon with me

i'm on the lower east side
in new york city
and i can't   i can't
talk witchu no more

    lady in yellow
we gotta dance to keep from cryin

    lady in brown
we gotta dance to keep from dyin

    lady in red
so come on

>   *lady in brown*
> come on
>
>   *lady in purple*
> come on
>
>   *lady in orange*
> hold yr head like it was ruby sapphire
> i'm a poet
> who writes in english
> come to share the worlds witchu
>
>   *everyone*
> come to share our worlds witchu
> we come here to be dancin
>   to be dancin
>   to be dancin
>   baya

There is a sudden light change, all of the ladies react as if they had been struck in the face. The lady in green and the lady in yellow run out up left, the lady in orange runs out the left volm, the lady in brown runs out up right.

16

>   *lady in blue*
a friend is hard to press charges against

>   *lady in red*
if you know him
you must have wanted it

>   *lady in purple*
a misunderstanding

>   *lady in red*
you know
these things happen

>   *lady in blue*
are you sure
you didnt suggest

>   *lady in purple*
had you been drinkin

>   *lady in red*
a rapist is always to be a stranger
to be legitimate
someone you never saw
a man wit obvious problems

17

lady in purple
pin-ups attached to the insides of his lapels

lady in blue
ticket stubs from porno flicks in his pocket

lady in purple
a lil dick

lady in red
or a strong mother

lady in blue
or just a brutal virgin

lady in red
but if you've been seen in public wit him
danced one dance
kissed him good-bye lightly

lady in purple
wit closed mouth

lady in blue
pressin charges will be as hard
as keepin yr legs closed
while five fools try to run a train on you

lady in red
these men friends of ours
who smile nice
stay employed
and take us out to dinner

lady in purple
lock the door behind you

lady in blue
wit fist in face
to fuck

lady in red
who make elaborate mediterranean dinners
& let the art ensemble carry all ethical burdens
while they invite a coupla friends over to have you
are sufferin from latent rapist bravado
& we are left wit the scars

lady in blue
bein betrayed by men who know us

lady in purple
& expect
like the stranger
we always thot waz comin

19

lady in blue
that we will submit

lady in purple
we must have known

lady in red
women relinquish all personal rights
in the presence of a man
who apparently cd be considered a rapist

lady in purple
especially if he has been considered a friend

lady in blue
& is no less worthy of bein beat witin an inch of his
        life
bein publicly ridiculed
havin two fists shoved up his ass

lady in red
than the stranger
we always thot it wd be

lady in blue
who never showed up

lady in red
cuz it turns out the nature of rape has changed

lady in blue
we can now meet them in circles we frequent for
     companionship

lady in purple
we see them at the coffeehouse

lady in blue
wit someone else we know

lady in red
we cd even have em over for dinner
& get raped in our own houses
by invitation
a friend

> *The lights change, and*
> *the ladies are all hit by an*
> *imaginary slap, the lady*
> *in red runs off up left.*

lady in blue
eyes

>   *lady in purple*
mice

>   *lady in blue*
womb

>   *lady in blue & lady in purple*
nobody

>   *The lady in purple exits up right.*

>   *lady in blue*
tubes tables white washed windows
grime from age wiped over once
legs spread
anxious
eyes crawling up on me
eyes rollin in my thighs
metal horses gnawin my womb
dead mice fall from my mouth
i really didnt mean to
i really didnt think i cd
just one day off . . .
get offa me alla this blood
bones shattered like soft ice-cream cones

i cdnt have people
lookin at me

pregnant
i cdnt have my friends see this
dyin danglin tween my legs
& i didnt say a thing
not a sigh
or a fast scream
to get
those eyes offa me
get them steel rods outta me
this hurts
this hurts me
& nobody came
cuz nobody knew
once i waz pregnant & shamed of myself.

*The lady in blue exits
stage left volm.*

*Soft deep music is heard,
voices calling "Sechita"
come from the wings and
volms. The lady in purple
enters from up right.*

lady in purple
once there were quadroon balls/elegance in st.
louis/laced

mulattoes/gamblin down the mississippi/to
     memphis/new
orleans n okra crepes near the bayou/where the
     poor white trash
wd sing/moanin/strange/liquid tones/thru the
     swamps

*The lady in green enters
from the right volm; she
is Sechita and for the rest
of the poem dances out
Sechita's life.*

sechita had heard these things/she moved as if she'd
known them/the silver n high-toned laughin/
the violins n marble floors/sechita pushed the clingin
delta dust wit painted toes/the patch-work tent waz
poka-dotted/stale lights snatched at the shadows/
creole carnival waz playin natchez in ten minutes/
her splendid red garters/gin-stained n itchy on her
thigh/blk-diamond stockings darned wit yellow
threads/an ol starched taffeta can-can fell abundantly
orange/from her waist round the splinterin chair/
sechita/egyptian/goddess of creativity/2nd
millennium/threw her heavy hair in a coil over her
neck/sechita/goddess/the recordin of history/

24

for colored girls who have considered suicide/
when the rainbow is enuf

sechita/ egyptian/ goddess of creativity/ 2nd millennium/
threw her heavy hair in a coil over her neck

she became herself/ ordinary/ brown braided
woman/ with big legs & full lips/ reglar

COME OVER HERE BITCH
CANT YA SEE THIS IS $5

i cdnt stand bein sorry & colored at the same time
it's so redundant in the modern world

i lived wit myths & music waz my ol man
& i cd dance a dance outta time

my spirit is
too ancient to
understand the
separation of soul
& gender /
my love is too
delicate to have
thrown back on
my face

oh sanctified/ oh sanctified/
and beautiful/ and beautiful

my stuff is the anonymous
ripped off treasure of the year

& he dropped em

spread crimson oil on her cheeks/waxed her
eyebrows/n unconsciously slugged the last hard
whiskey in the glass/the broken mirror she used to
decorate her face/made her forehead tilt backwards/
her cheeks appear sunken/her sassy chin only large
enuf/to keep her full lower lip/from growin into her
neck/sechita/had learned to make allowances for
the distortions/but the heavy dust of the delta/left a
tinge of grit n darkness/on every one of her dresses/
on her arms & her shoulders/sechita/waz anxious
to get back to st. louis/the dirt there didnt crawl
from the earth into yr soul/at least/in st. louis/the
grime waz store bought second-hand/here in
natchez/god seemed to be wipin his feet in her face/

one of the wrestlers had finally won tonite/the
mulatto/raul/was sposed to hold the boomin half-
caste/searin eagle/in a bear hug/8 counts/get
thrown unawares/fall out the ring/n then do searin
eagle in for good/sechita/cd hear redneck whoops n
slappin on the back/she gathered her sparsely
sequined skirts/tugged the waist cincher from under
her greyin slips/n made her face immobile/she made
her face like nefertiti/approachin her own tomb/
she suddenly threw/her leg full-force/thru the
canvas curtain/a deceptive glass stone/sparkled/
malignant on her ankle/her calf waz tauntin in the

brazen carnie lights/the full moon/sechita/goddess/
of love/egypt/2nd millennium/performin the rites/
the conjurin of men/conjurin the spirit/in natchez/
the mississippi spewed a heavy fume of barely movin
waters/sechita's legs slashed furiously thru the
cracker nite/& gold pieces hittin the makeshift
stage/her thighs/they were aimin coins tween her
thighs/sechita/egypt/goddess/harmony/kicked
viciously thru the nite/catchin stars tween her toes.

The lady in green exits into
the stage left volm, the
lady in purple exits into
up stage left.

The lady in brown enters
from up stage right.

    lady in brown
de library waz right down from de trolly tracks
cross from de laundry-mat
thru de big shinin floors & granite pillars
ol st. louis is famous for
i found toussaint
but not til after months uv
cajun katie/pippi longstockin
christopher robin/eddie heyward & a pooh bear

in the children's room
only pioneer girls & magic rabbits
& big city white boys
i knew i waznt sposedta
but i ran inta the ADULT READING ROOM
       & came across

TOUSSAINT

       my first blk man
(i never counted george washington carver
cuz i didnt like peanuts)
        still
TOUSSAINT waz a blk man a negro like my mama
    say
who refused to be a slave
& he spoke french
& didnt low no white man to tell him nothin
        not napolean
        not maximillien
        not robespierre

TOUSSAINT L'OUVERTURE
waz the beginnin uv reality for me
in the summer contest for
who colored child can read
15 books in three weeks

27

i won & raved abt TOUSSAINT L'OUVERTURE
at the afternoon ceremony
waz disqualified
      cuz Toussaint
         belonged in the ADULT READING ROOM
         & i cried
& carried dead Toussaint home in the book
he waz dead & livin to me
cuz TOUSSAINT & them
they held the citadel gainst the french
wid the spirits of ol dead africans from outta the
    ground
TOUSSAINT led they army of zombies
walkin cannon ball shootin spirits to free Haiti
& they waznt slaves no more

              TOUSSAINT L'OUVERTURE
became my secret lover at the age of 8
i entertained him in my bedroom
widda flashlight under my covers
way inta the night/we discussed strategies
how to remove white girls from my hopscotch games
& etc.
TOUSSAINT
waz layin in bed wit me next to raggedy ann
the night i decided to run away from my
        integrated home

                    integrated street
                    integrated school
1955 waz not a good year for lil blk girls

Toussaint said 'lets go to haiti'
i said 'awright'
& packed some very important things in a brown
        paper bag
so i wdnt haveta come back
then Toussaint & i took the hodiamont streetcar
to the river
last stop
only 15¢
cuz there waznt nobody cd see Toussaint cept me
& we walked all down thru north st. louis
where the french settlers usedta live
in tiny brick houses all huddled together
wit barely missin windows & shingles uneven
wit colored kids playin & women on low porches
        sippin beer

i cd talk to Toussaint down by the river
like this waz where we waz gonna stow away
on a boat for new orleans
& catch a creole fishin-rig for port-au-prince
then we waz just gonna read & talk all the time
& eat fried bananas

we waz just walkin & skippin past ol
drunk men
when dis ol young boy jumped out at me sayin
'HEY GIRL YA BETTAH COME OVAH HEAH N
TALK TO ME'
well
i turned to TOUSSAINT (who waz furious)
& i shouted
'ya silly ol boy
ya bettah leave me alone
or TOUSSAINT'S gonna get yr ass'
de silly ol boy came round de corner laughin all in
my face
'yellah gal
ya sure must be somebody to know my name so
quick'
i waz disgusted
& wanted to get on to haiti
widout some tacky ol boy botherin me
still he kept standin there
kickin milk cartons & bits of brick
tryin to get all in my business
i mumbled to L'OUVERTURE 'what shd I do'
finally
i asked this silly ol boy
'WELL WHO ARE YOU?'
he say

'MY NAME IS TOUSSAINT JONES'
well
i looked right at him
those skidded out cordoroy pants
a striped teashirt wid holes in both elbows
a new scab over his left eye
& i said
    'what's yr name again'
he say
'i'm toussaint jones'
'wow
i am on my way to see
TOUSSAINT L'OUVERTURE in HAITI
are ya any kin to him
he dont take no stuff from no white folks
& they gotta country all they own
& there aint no slaves'
that silly ol boy squinted his face all up
'looka heah girl
i am TOUSSAINT JONES
& i'm right heah lookin at ya
& i dont take no stuff from no white folks
ya dont see none round heah do ya?'
& he sorta pushed out his chest
then he say
'come on lets go on down to the docks
& look at the boats'

i waz real puzzled goin down to the docks
wit my paper bag & my books
i felt TOUSSAINT L'OUVERTURE sorta leave me
& i waz sad
til i realized
TOUSSAINT JONES waznt too different
from TOUSSAINT L'OUVERTURE
cept the ol one waz in haiti
& this one wid me speakin english & eatin apples
yeah.
toussaint jones waz awright wit me
no tellin what all spirits we cd move
down by the river
st. louis 1955   hey wait.

> *The lady in brown exits*
> *into the stage right volm.*

> *The lady in red enters*
> *from the stage left volm.*

   lady in red
orange butterflies & aqua sequins
ensconsed tween slight bosoms
silk roses dartin from behind her ears
the passion flower of southwest los angeles
meandered down hoover street

past dark shuttered houses where
women from louisiana shelled peas
round 3:00 & sent their sons
whistlin to the store for fatback & black-eyed peas
she glittered in heat
& seemed to be lookin for rides
when she waznt & absolutely
eyed every man who waznt lame white or noddin out
she let her thigh slip from her skirt
crossin the street
she slowed to be examined
& she never looked back to smile
or acknowledge a sincere 'hey mama'
or to meet the eyes of someone
purposely findin sometin to do in
her direction

       she waz sullen
       & the rhinestones etchin the corners of
         her mouth
       suggested tears
       fresh kisses that had done no good
she always wore her stomach out
lined with small iridescent feathers
the hairs round her navel seemed to dance
& she didnt let on
she knew
from behind her waist waz aching to be held

the pastel ivy drawn on her shoulders
to be brushed with lips & fingers
smellin of honey & jack daniels
        she waz hot
        a deliberate coquette
        who never did without
        what she wanted
& she wanted to be unforgettable
she wanted to be a memory
a wound   to every man
arragant enough to want her
        she waz the wrath
         of women in windows
           fingerin shades/ol lace curtains
            camoflagin despair &
              stretch marks
so she glittered honestly
delighted she waz desired
& allowed those especially
schemin/tactful suitors
to experience her body & spirit
tearin/so easily blendin with theirs/
& they were so happy
& lay on her lime sheets full & wet
from her tongue   she kissed
them reverently   even ankles
edges of beards . . .

The stage goes to darkness
except for a special on the
lady in red, who lies
motionless on the floor;
as the lights slowly fade
up the lady in red sits up.

at 4:30 AM
she rose
movin the arms & legs that trapped her
she sighed affirmin the sculptured man
& made herself a bath
of dark musk oil egyptian crystals
& florida water to remove his smell
to wash away the glitter
to watch the butterflies melt into
suds & the rhinestones fall beneath
her buttocks like smooth pebbles
in a missouri creek
layin in water
she became herself
ordinary
brown braided woman
with big legs & full lips
reglar
seriously intendin to finish her

night's work
she quickly walked to her guest
straddled on her pillows & began
            'you'll have to go now/i've
            a lot of work to do/& i cant
            with a man around/here are yr pants/
            there's coffee on the stove/its been
            very nice/but i cant see you again/
            you got what you came for/didnt you'
& she smiled
he wd either mumble curses bout crazy bitches
or sit dumbfounded
while she repeated
            'i cdnt possibly wake up/with
            a strange man in my bed/why
            dont you go home'
she cda been slapped upside the head
or verbally challenged
but she never waz
& the ones who fell prey to the
dazzle of hips painted with
orange blossoms & magnolia scented wrists
had wanted no more
than to lay between her sparklin thighs
& had planned on leavin before dawn
& she had been so divine
devastatingly bizarre the way

her mouth fit round
& now she stood a
reglar colored girl
fulla the same malice
livid indifference as a sistah
worn from supportin a wd be hornplayer
or waitin by the window
        & they knew
        & left in a hurry
she wd gather her tinsel &
jewels from the tub
& laugh gayly or vengeful
she stored her silk roses by her bed
& when she finished writin
the account of her exploit in a diary
embroidered with lilies & moonstones
she placed the rose behind her ear
& cried herself to sleep.

All the lights fade except
for a special on the lady
in red; the lady in red
exits into the stage left
volm.

The lady in blue enters
from up right.

lady in blue
i usedta live in the world
then i moved to HARLEM
& my universe is now six blocks

when i walked in the pacific
i imagined waters ancient from accra/tunis
cleansin me/feedin me
now my ankles are coated in grey filth
from the puddle neath the hydrant

my oceans were life
what waters i have here sit stagnant
circlin ol men's bodies
shit & broken lil whiskey bottles
left to make me bleed

i usedta live in the world
now i live in harlem & my universe is six blocks
a tunnel with a train
i can ride anywhere
remaining a stranger

> NO MAN YA CANT GO WIT ME/I DONT
> EVEN KNOW YOU/NO/I DONT WANNA
> KISS YOU/YOU AINT BUT 12 YRS OLD/
> NO MAN/PLEASE PLEASE PLEASE LEAVE
> ME ALONE/TOMORROW/YEAH/NO/
> PLEASE/I CANT USE IT

i cd stay alone
a woman in the world
then i moved to
HARLEM
i come in at dusk
stay close to the curb

> *The lady in yellow enters,*
> *she's waiting for a bus.*

round midnite
praying wont no young man
think i'm pretty in a dark mornin

> *The lady in purple enters,*
> *she's waiting for a bus.*

wdnt be good
not good at all
to meet a tall short black brown young man fulla
    his power
in the dark
in my universe of six blocks
straight up brick walls
women hangin outta windows
like ol silk stockings
cats cryin/children gigglin/a tavern wit red curtains

39

bad smells/kissin ladies smilin & dirt
sidewalks spittin/men cursing/playin

> *The lady in orange enters,*
> *she is being followed by*
> *a man, the lady in blue*
> *becomes that man.*

'I SPENT MORE MONEY YESTERDAY
THAN THE DAY BEFORE & ALL THAT'S
MORE N YOU NIGGAH EVER GOTTA
HOLD TO COME OVER HERE BITCH
CANT YA SEE THIS IS $5'

never mind sister
dont play him no mind
go go go go go go sister
do yr thing
never mind

i usedta live in the world
really be in the world
free & sweet talkin
good mornin & thank-you & nice day
uh huh
i cant now
i cant be nice to nobody
nice is such a rip-off

reglar beauty & a smile in the street
is just a set-up

i usedta be in the world
a woman in the world
i hadda right to the world
then i moved to harlem
for the set-up
a universe
six blocks of cruelty
piled up on itself
a tunnel
closin

*The four ladies on stage
freeze, count 4, then the
ladies in blue, purple,
yellow and orange move to
their places for the next
poem.*

    lady in purple
three of us like a pyramid
three friends
one laugh
one music
one flowered shawl
knotted on each neck

41

we all saw him at the same time
& he saw us
i felt a quick thump in each one of us
didnt know what to do
we all wanted what waz comin our way
so we split
but he found one
& she loved him

the other two were tickled
& spurned his advances
when the one who loved him waz somewhere else
he wd come to her saying
yr friends love you very much
i have tried
& they keep askin where are you
she smiled
wonderin how long her friends
wd hold out
he waz what they were lookin for
he bided his time
he waited til romance waned
the three of us made up stories
bout usedta & cda been nice
the season waz dry
no men
no quickies

not one dance or eyes unrelentin
one day after another
cept for the one who loved him
he appeared irregularly
expectin graciousness no matter what
she cut fresh strawberries
her friends callt less frequently
went on hunts for passin fancies
she cdnt figure out what waz happenin
then the rose
she left by his pillow
she found on her friends desk
& there waz nothing to say
she said
i wanna tell you
he's been after me
all the time
says he's free & can explain
what's happenin wit you
is nothin to me
& i dont wanna hurt you
but you know i need someone now
& you know
how wonderful he is
her friend cdnt speak or cry
they hugged & went to where he waz
wit another woman

he said good-bye to one
tol the other he wd call
he smiled a lot

she held her head on her lap
the lap of her sisters soakin up tears
each understandin how much love stood between
        them
how much love between them
love between them
love like sisters

> *Sharp music is heard,*
> *each lady dances as if*
> *catching a disease from*
> *the lady next to her,*
> *suddenly they all freeze.*

   lady in orange
ever since i realized there waz someone callt
a colored girl an evil woman a bitch or a nag
i been tryin not to be that & leave bitterness
in somebody else's cup/come to somebody to love me
without deep & nasty smellin scald from lye or bein
left screamin in a street fulla lunatics/whisperin
slut bitch bitch niggah/get outta here wit alla that/
i didnt have any of that for you/i brought you what
joy i found & i found joy/honest fingers round my

44

face/with dead musicians on 78's from cuba/or live
musicians on five dollar lp's from chicago/where i
have never been/& i love willie colon & arsenio
rodriquez/especially cuz i can make the music loud
enuf/so there is no me but dance/& when i can
dance like that/there's nothin cd hurt me/but i get
tired & i haveta come offa the floor & then there's
that woman who hurt you/who you left/three or
four times/& just went back/after you put my heart
in the bottom of yr shoe/you just walked back to
where you hurt/& i didnt have nothin/so i went to
where somebody had somethin for me/but he waznt
you/& i waz on the way back from her house in
the bottom of yr shoe/so this is not a love poem/
cuz there are only memorial albums available/& even
charlie mingus wanted desperately to be a pimp/
& i wont be able to see eddie palmieri for months/
so this is a requium for myself/cuz i have died in a
real way/not wid aqua coffins & du-wop cadillacs/
i used to joke abt when i waz messin round/but a
real dead lovin is here for you now/cuz i dont know
anymore/how to avoid my own face wet wit my
tears/cuz i had convinced myself colored girls had no
right to sorrow/& i lived & loved that way & kept
sorrow on the curb/allegedly for you/but i know i did
it for myself/
i cdnt stand it

i cdnt stand bein sorry & colored at the same time
it's so redundant in the modern world

lady in purple
i lived wit myths & music waz my ol man & i cd
dance a dance outta time/a dance wit no partners/
take my pills & keep right on steppin/linger in
non-english speakin arms so there waz no possibility
of understandin
& you YOU
came sayin i am the niggah/i am the baddest
muthafuckah out there/
i said yes/this is who i am waitin for
& to come wit you/i hadta bring everythin
the dance & the terror
the dead musicians & the hope
& those scars i had hidden wit smiles & good fuckin
lay open
& i dont know i dont know any more tricks
i am really colored & really sad sometimes & you hurt
me more than i ever danced outta/into oblivion isnt far
enuf to get outta this/i am ready to die like a lily in the
desert/& i cdnt let you in on it cuz i didnt know/here
is what i have/poems/big thighs/lil tits/& so much
love/will you take it from me this one time/please
this is for you/arsenio's tres cleared the way & makes
me pure again/please please/this is for you i want

you to love me/let me love you/i dont wanna dance
wit ghosts/snuggle lovers i made up in my
drunkenness/lemme love you just like i am/a colored
girl/i'm finally bein real/no longer symmetrical &
impervious to pain

    lady in blue
we deal wit emotion too much
so why dont we go on ahead & be white then/
& make everythin dry & abstract wit no rhythm & no
reelin for sheer sensual pleasure/yes let's go on & be
white/we're right in the middle of it/no use holdin
out/holdin onto ourselves/lets think our way outta
feelin/lets abstract ourselves some families & maybe
maybe tonite/i'll find a way to make myself come
witout you/no fingers or other objects just thot which
isnt spiritual evolution cuz its empty & godliness is
plenty is ripe & fertile/thinkin wont do me a bit of
good tonite/i need to be loved/& havent the audacity
to say
where are you/& dont know who to say it to

    lady in yellow
i've lost it
touch wit reality/i dont know who's doin it
i thot i waz but i waz so stupid i waz able to be hurt
& that's not real/not anymore/i shd be immune/if
i'm still alive & that's what i waz discussin/how i am

still alive & my dependency on other livin beins for
love i survive on intimacy & tomorrow/that's all i've
got goin & the music waz like smack & you knew abt
that & still refused my dance waz not enuf/& it waz
all i had but bein alive & bein a woman & bein
colored is a metaphysical dilemma/i havent conquered
yet/do you see the point my spirit is too ancient to
understand the separation of soul & gender/my love
is too delicate to have thrown back on my face

> *The ladies in red, green,
> and brown enter quietly;
> in the background all of
> the ladies except the lady
> in yellow are frozen; the
> lady in yellow looks at
> them, walks by them,
> touches them; they do not
> move.*

    lady in yellow
my love is too delicate to have thrown back on my
    face

> *The lady in yellow starts
> to exit into the stage right
> volm. Just as she gets to
> the volm, the lady in
> brown comes to life.*

lady in brown

my love is too beautiful to have thrown back on my
       face

lady in purple

my love is too sanctified to have thrown back on
       my face

lady in blue

my love is too magic to have thrown back on my face

lady in orange

my love is too saturday nite to have thrown back
       on my face

lady in red

my love is too complicated to have thrown back on
       my face

lady in green

my love is too music to have thrown back on my face

everyone

music

music

*The lady in green then
breaks into a dance, the
other ladies follow her
lead and soon they are all
dancing and chanting
together.*

　　lady in green
yank dankka dank dank

　　everyone
music

　　lady in green
yank dankka dank dank

　　everyone
music

　　lady in green
yank dankka dank dank

　　everyone (but started by the lady in yellow)
delicate
delicate
delicate

  everyone (but started by the lady in brown)
and beautiful
and beautiful
and beautiful

  everyone (but started by the lady in purple)
oh sanctified
oh sanctified
oh sanctified

  everyone (but started by the lady in blue)
magic
magic
magic

  everyone (but started by the lady in orange)
and saturday nite
and saturday nite
and saturday nite

  everyone (but started by the lady in red)
and complicated
and complicated
and complicated
and complicated
and complicated

and complicated
and complicated
and complicated

> *The dance reaches a
> climax and all of the ladies
> fall out tired, but full of
> life and togetherness.*

   lady in green

somebody almost walked off wid alla my stuff
not my poems or a dance i gave up in the street
but somebody almost walked off wid alla my stuff
like a kleptomaniac workin hard & forgettin while
stealin
this is mine/this aint yr stuff/
now why dont you put me back & let me hang out in
my own self
somebody almost walked off wid alla my stuff
& didnt care enuf to send a note home sayin'
i waz late for my solo conversation
or two sizes too small for my own tacky skirts
what can anybody do wit somethin of no value on a
open market/did you getta dime for my things/hey
man/where are you goin wid alla my stuff/this is a
woman's trip & i need my stuff/to ohh & ahh abt/

daddy/i gotta mainline number from my own shit/
now wontchu put me back/& let me play this duet/wit
this silver ring in my nose/honest to god/somebody
almost run off wit alla my stuff/& i didnt bring anythin
but the kick & sway of it the perfect ass for my man &
none of it is theirs this is mine/ntozake 'her own
things'/that's my name/now give me my stuff/i see
ya hidin my laugh/& how i sit wif my legs open
sometimes/to give my crotch some sunlight/& there
goes my love my toes my chewed up finger nails/
niggah/wif the curls in yr hair/mr. louisiana hot link/
i want my stuff back/my rhythms & my voice/open
my mouth/& let me talk ya outta/throwin my shit
in the sewar/this is some delicate leg & whimsical
kiss/i gotta have to give to my choice/without you
runnin off wit alla my shit/now you cant have me
less i give me away/& i waz doin all that/til ya run
off on a good thing/who is this you left me wit/
some simple bitch widda bad attitude/i wants my
things/i want my arm wit the hot iron scar/& my
leg wit the flea bite/i want my calloused feet & quik
language back in my mouth/fried plantains/
pineapple pear juice/sun-ra & joseph & jules/i want
my own things/how i lived them/& give me my
memories/how i waz when i waz there/you cant
have them or do nothin wit them/stealin my shit
from me/dont make it yrs/makes it stolen/somebody

almost run off wit alla my stuff/& i waz standin
there/lookin at myself/the whole time & it waznt
a spirit took my stuff/waz a man whose ego walked
round like Rodan's shadow/waz a man faster n my
innocence/waz a lover/i made too much room for/
almost run off wit alla my stuff/& i didnt know i'd
give it up so quik/& the one running wit it/dont
know he got it/& i'm shoutin this is mine/& he dont
know he got it/my stuff is the anonymous ripped off
treasure of the year/did you know somebody almost
got away with me/me in a plastic bag under their
arm/me danglin on a string of personal carelessness/
i'm spattered wit mud & city rain/& no i didnt get
a chance to take a douche/hey man/this is not your
perogative/i gotta have me in my pocket/to get
round like a good woman shd/& make the poem in
the pot or the chicken in the dance/what i got to do/
i gotta have my stuff to do it to/why dont ya find
yr own things/& leave this package of me for my
destiny/what ya got to get from me/i'll give it to ya/
yeh/i'll give it to ya/round 5:00 in the winter/
when the sky is blue-red/& Dew City is gettin
pressed/if it's really my stuff/ya gotta give it to me/
if ya really want it/i'm the only one/can handle it

 lady in blue
that niggah will be back tomorrow, sayin 'i'm sorry'

lady in yellow
get this, last week my ol man came in sayin, 'i don't
know how she got yr number baby, i'm sorry'

lady in brown
no this one is it, 'o baby, ya know i waz high, i'm
sorry'

lady in purple
'i'm only human, and inadequacy is what makes us
human, & if we was perfect we wdnt have nothin to
strive for, so you might as well go on and forgive
me pretty baby, cause i'm sorry'

lady in green
'shut up bitch, i told you i waz sorry'

lady in orange
no this one is it, 'i do ya like i do ya cause i thot
ya could take it, now i'm sorry'

lady in red
'now i know that ya know i love ya, but i aint ever
gonna love ya like ya want me to love ya, i'm sorry'

lady in blue
one thing i dont need
is any more apologies
i got sorry greetin me at my front door
you can keep yrs
i dont know what to do wit em
they dont open doors
or bring the sun back
they dont make me happy
or get a mornin paper
didnt nobody stop usin my tears to wash cars
cuz a sorry

i am simply tired
of collectin
                i didnt know
                i was so important toyou'
i'm gonna haveta throw some away
i cant get to the clothes in my closet
for alla the sorries
i'm gonna tack a sign to my door
leave a message by the phone
                'if you called
                to say yr sorry
                call somebody
                else
                i dont use em anymore'

i let sorry/didnt meanta/& how cd i know abt that
take a walk down a dark & musty street in brooklyn
i'm gonna do exactly what i want to
& i wont be sorry for none of it
letta sorry soothe yr soul/i'm gonna soothe mine

you were always inconsistent
doin somethin & then bein sorry
beatin my heart to death
talkin bout you sorry
well
i will not call
i'm not goin to be nice
i will raise my voice
& scream & holler
& break things & race the engine
& tell all yr secrets bout yrself to yr face
& i will list in detail everyone of my wonderful lovers
& their ways
i will play oliver lake
loud
& i wont be sorry for none of it

i loved you on purpose
i was open on purpose
i still crave vulnerability & close talk
& i'm not even sorry bout you bein sorry

you can carry all the guilt & grime ya wanna
just dont give it to me
i cant use another sorry
next time
you should admit
you're mean/low-down/triflin/& no count straight
    out
steada bein sorry alla the time
enjoy bein yrself

    lady in red
there waz no air/the sheets made ripples under his
body like crumpled paper napkins in a summer park/,
& lil specks of somethin from tween his toes or the
biscuits from the day before ran in the sweat that
tucked the sheet into his limbs like he waz an ol
frozen bundle of chicken/& he'd get up to make
coffee, drink wine, drink water/he wished one of his
friends who knew where he waz wd come by with
some blow or some shit/anythin/there waz no air/
he'd see the spotlights in the alleyways downstairs
movin in the air/cross his wall over his face/& get
under the covers & wait for an all clear or til he cd
hear traffic again/.

there waznt nothin wrong with him/there waznt
nothin wrong with him/he kept tellin crystal/any

niggah wanna kill vietnamese children more n stay
home & raise his own is sicker than a rabid dog/that's
how their thing had been goin since he got back/
crystal just got inta sayin whatta fool niggah beau waz
& always had been/didnt he go all over uptown sayin
the child waznt his/waz some no counts bastard/&
any ol city police cd come & get him if they wanted/
cuz as soon as the blood type & shit waz together/
everybody wd know that crystal waz a no good lyin
whore/and this after she'd been his girl since she waz
thirteen/when he caught her on the stairway/

he came home crazy as hell/he tried to get veterans
benefits to go to school & they kept right on puttin
him in remedial classes/he cdnt read wortha damn/so
beau cused the teachers of holdin him back & got
himself a gypsy cab to drive/but his cab kept breakin
down/& the cops was always messin wit him/plus not
gettin much bread/

& crystal went & got pregnant again/beau most beat
her to death when she tol him/she still gotta scar
under her right tit where he cut her up/still crystal
went right on & had the baby/so now beau willie had
two children/a little girl/naomi kenya & a boy/
kwame beau willie brown/& there waz no air/

how in the hell did he get in this mess anyway/
somebody went & tol crystal that beau waz spendin
alla his money on the bartendin bitch down at the
merry-go-round cafe/beau sat straight up in the bed/
wrapped up in the sheets lookin like john the baptist
or a huge baby wit stubble & nuts/now he hadta get
alla that shit outta crystal's mind/so she wd let him
come home/crystal had gone & got a court order
saying beau willie brown had no access to his
children/if he showed his face he waz subject to
arrest/shit/she'd been in his ass to marry her since
she waz 14 years old & here when she 22/she wanna
throw him out cuz he say he'll marry her/she burst
out laughin/hollerin whatchu wanna marry me for
now/so i can support yr ass/or come sit wit ya when
they lock yr behind up/cause they gonna come for
ya/ya goddamn lunatic/they gonna come/& i'm not
gonna have a thing to do wit it/o no i wdnt marry yr
pitiful black ass for nothin & she went on to bed/

the next day beau willie came in blasted & got ta
swingin chairs at crystal/who cdnt figure out what the
hell he waz doin/til he got ta shoutin bout how she
waz gonna marry him/& get some more veterans
benefits/& he cd stop drivin them crazy spics round/
while they tryin to kill him for $15/beau waz sweatin
terrible/beatin on crystal/& he cdnt do no more with

the table n chairs/so he went to get the high chair/&
lil kwame waz in it/& beau waz beatin crystal with
the high chair & her son/& some notion got inta him
to stop/and he run out/

crystal most died/that's why the police wdnt low
beau near where she lived/& she'd been tellin the kids
their daddy tried to kill her & kwame/& he just
wanted to marry her/that's what/he wanted to marry
her/& have a family/but the bitch waz crazy/beau
willie waz sittin in this hotel in his drawers drinkin
coffee & wine in the heat of the day spillin shit all over
hisself/laughin/bout how he waz gonna get crystal to
take him back/& let him be a man in the house/&
she wdnt even have to go to work no more/he got
dressed all up in his ivory shirt & checkered pants to
go see crystal & get this mess all cleared up/he
knocked on the door to crystal's rooms/& she didnt
answer/he beat on the door & crystal & naomi started
cryin/beau gotta shoutin again how he wanted to
marry her/& waz she always gonna be a whore/or did
she wanna husband/& crystal just kept on screamin
for him to leave us alone/just leave us alone/so beau
broke the door down/crystal held the children in
fronta her/she picked kwame off the floor/in her
arms/& she held naomi by her shoulders/& kept on
sayin/beau willie brown/get outta here/the police is

gonna come for ya/ya fool/get outta here/do you
want the children to see you act the fool again/you
want kwame to brain damage from you throwin him
round/niggah/get outta here/get out & dont show yr
ass again or i'll kill ya/i swear i'll kill ya/he reached
for naomi/crystal grabbed the lil girl & stared at beau
willie like he waz a leper or somethin/dont you touch
my children/muthafucker/or i'll kill you/

beau willie jumped back all humble & apologetic/i'm
sorry/i dont wanna hurt em/i just wanna hold em &
get on my way/i dont wanna cuz you no more
trouble/i wanted to marry you & give ya things
what you gonna give/a broken jaw/niggah get outta
here/he ignored crystal's outburst & sat down motionin
for naomi to come to him/she smiled back at her
daddy/ crystal felt naomi givin in & held her tighter/
naomi/pushed away & ran to her daddy/cryin/daddy,
daddy come back daddy/come back/but be nice to
mommy/cause mommy loves you/and ya gotta be
nice/he sat her on his knee/& played with her ribbons
& they counted fingers & toes/every so often he
looked over to crystal holdin kwame/like a statue/&
he'd say/see crystal/i can be a good father/now let
me see my son/ & she didnt move/& he coaxed her &
he coaxed her/tol her she waz still a hot lil ol thing &
pretty & strong/didnt she get right up after that lil ol

fight they had & go back to work/beau willie oozed
kindness & crystal who had known so lil/let beau
hold kwame/

as soon as crystal let the baby outta her arms/beau
jumped up a laughin & a gigglin/a hootin & a
hollerin/awright bitch/awright bitch/you gonna
marry me/you gonna marry me . . .
i aint gonna marry ya/i aint ever gonna marry ya/for
nothin/you gonna be in the jail/you gonna be under
the jail for this/now gimme my kids/ya give me
back my kids/

he kicked the screen outta the window/& held the
kids offa the sill/you gonna marry me/yeh, i'll marry
ya/anything/but bring the children back in the
house/he looked from where the kids were hangin
from the fifth story/at alla the people screamin at
him/& he started sweatin again/say to alla the
neighbors/you gonna marry me/

i stood by beau in the window/with naomi reachin for
me/& kwame screamin mommy mommy from the
fifth story/but i cd only whisper/& he dropped em

    lady in red
i waz missin somethin

lady in purple
somethin so important

lady in orange
somethin promised

lady in blue
a layin on of hands

lady in green
fingers near my forehead

lady in yellow
strong

lady in green
cool

lady in orange
movin

lady in purple
makin me whole

lady in orange
sense

> *lady in green*
> pure

> *lady in blue*
> all the gods comin into me
> layin me open to myself

> *lady in red*
> i waz missin somethin

> *lady in green*
> somethin promised

> *lady in orange*
> somethin free

> *lady in purple*
> a layin on of hands

> *lady in blue*
> i know bout/layin on bodies/layin outta man
> bringin him alla my fleshy self & some of my pleasure
> bein taken full eager wet like i get sometimes
> i waz missin somethin

> *lady in purple*
> a layin on of hands

> *lady in blue*
> not a man
>
> *lady in yellow*
> layin on
>
> *lady in purple*
> not my mama/holdin me tight/sayin
> i'm always gonna be her girl
> not a layin on of bosom & womb
> a layin on of hands
> the holiness of myself released
>
> *lady in red*
> i sat up one nite walkin a boardin house
> screamin/cryin/the ghost of another woman
> who waz missin what i waz missin
> i wanted to jump up outta my bones
> & be done wit myself
> leave me alone
> & go on in the wind
> it waz too much
> i fell into a numbness
> til the only tree i cd see
> took me up in her branches
> held me in the breeze
> made me dawn dew

that chill at daybreak
the sun wrapped me up swingin rose light everywhere
the sky laid over me like a million men
i waz cold/i waz burnin up/a child
& endlessly weavin garments for the moon
wit my tears

i found god in myself
& i loved her/i loved her fiercely

> All of the ladies repeat to
> themselves softly the lines
> 'i found god in myself & i
> loved her.' It soon becomes
> a song of joy, started by
> the lady in blue. The ladies
> sing first to each other,
> then gradually to the
> audience. After the song
> peaks the ladies enter into
> a closed tight circle.

lady in brown
& this is for colored girls who have considered
suicide/but are movin to the ends of their own
rainbows

ABOUT THE AUTHOR

NTOZAKE SHANGE is the author of *Nappy Edges* and *Sassafras*. She has written for *Black Scholar, Yardbird Reader, Invisible City, Third World Woman, Time to Greez, Margins, Black Maria, West End* magazine, *Broadway Boogie, APR* and *Shocks*. Her play *A Photograph: A Still Life With Shadows/A Photograph: A Study in Cruelty* was produced by The Public Theatre in New York City in the winter of 1977. Along with Jessica Hagedorn and Thulani ("The Satin Sisters") she wrote and performed in *Where the Mississippi Meets the Amazon* presented by Joseph Papp at the Public Theatre Cabaret. Her latest play, *Spell #7* was presented at the Public Theatre in the summer of 1979. Ms. Shange currently lives in New York City.

DISCOVER
THE DRAMA OF LIFE
IN THE LIFE OF DRAMA

]	13434	**CYRANO DE BERGERAC** Edmond Rostand	$1.75
]	21040	**FOUR GREAT PLAYS** Henrik Ibsen	$2.25
]	13615	**COMP. PLAYS SOPHOCLES**	$2.95
]	20459	**FOR COLORED GIRLS WHO HAVE CONSIDERED SUICIDE WHEN THE RAINBOW IS ENUF** Ntozake Shange	$2.75
]	14559	**MODERN AMERICAN SCENES FOR STUDENT ACTORS** Wynn Handman	$3.50
]	14257	**SAM SHEPARD: SEVEN PLAYS** Sam Shepard	$3.50
]	14674	**THE NIGHT THOREAU SPENT IN JAIL** Jerome Lawrence and Robert E. Lee	$2.25
]	12832	**THE PRICE** Arthur Miller	$1.95
]	14964	**BRIAN'S SONG** William Blinn	$2.25
]	14678	**THE EFFECTS OF GAMMA RAYS ON MAN-IN-THE-MOON MARIGOLDS** Paul Zindel	$2.25
]	14161	**50 GREAT SCENES FOR STUDENT ACTORS** Lewy Olfson, ed.	$2.50
]	14467	**INHERIT THE WIND** Lawrence & Lee	$1.95
]	13102	**TEN PLAYS BY EURIPIDES** Moses Hadas, ed.	$2.50
]	13902	**THE CRUCIBLE** Arthur Miller	$2.25
]	14689	**THE MIRACLE WORKER,** William Gibson	$2.25
]	14101	**AFTER THE FALL** Arthur Miller	$2.50